MW01617956

Printed in the United States of America

First Printing, 2016

ISBN 9780979620010

Status Symbol Publishing, LLC
289 Jonesboro Road, Ste. 195
McDonough, GA 30253

statussymbolpublishing@gmail.com

Mingo Mango the Flamingo and the Magic Rainbow

By Vele Keyta Y. Redding
Illustrated by Mao Zi Qiang

For Morgan

Mingo Mango is
his name.

He loves to play
out in the rain.

When it rains, he's
never blue.
It's his favorite thing
to do.

Splishing, splashing,
slipping, sliding…
Jumping in puddles
is so exciting.

As the sun begins
to shine,
And the rain
starts to leave —

**What to his wandering eyes
did Mingo Mango see?**

**A multicolored rainbow, stretching
from the sky to the sea.**

He had never seen anything quite… as brilliant, as radiant, as beautiful, as bright!

Red, yellow, blue and green…

Mingo Mango
thought, 'Is this
a dream?'

The rainbow smiled, then said "Hello."
"I'm a magic rainbow,"
as she cast her glow.

"Upon my colors make a wish —
That's all you have to do.

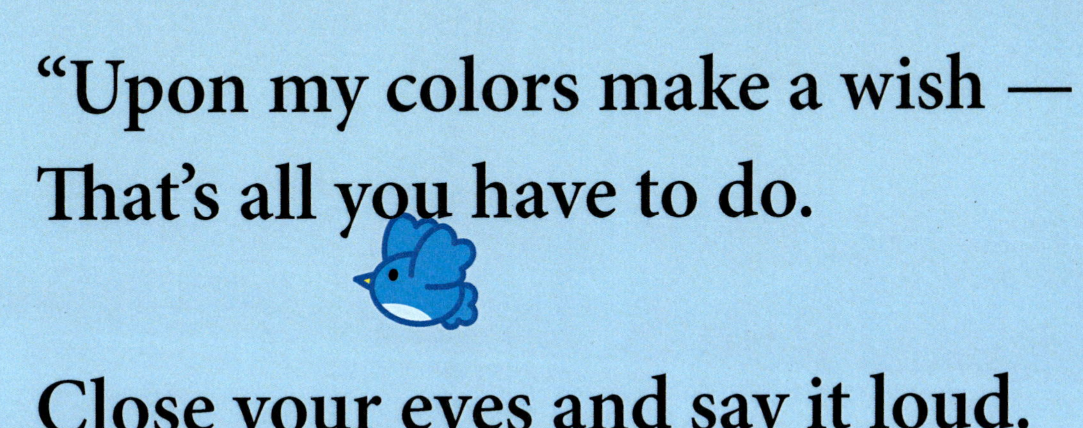

Close your eyes and say it loud.
Your wish will surely come true."

Closing his eyes and
squeezing them tight,
Mingo Mango wished
aloud with all his might.

"I wish upon the color red —
To give life to my flowerbed."

He opened his eyes,
and wouldn't you know
His wish had come true!
It was so.

Closing his eyes and squeezing
them tight,

Mingo Mango wished a second time
with all his might.

"I wish upon the color yellow —
To seed the grasslands in the
meadow."

Opening his eyes to the
rainbow's glow,

Mingo Mango's wish had come true!
And, it was so.

Closing his eyes and squeezing
them tight,

Mingo Mango wished a third time
with all his might.

"I wish upon the color blue —
To fill the air with gentle dew."

Mingo Mango opened his
eyes really slow,

Peering into the rainbow's glow,
his wish had come true!
And, it was so.

Closing his eyes and
squeezing them tight,

Mingo Mango wished a fourth
time with all his might.

"I wish upon the color green —
For an earth lush and pristine."

Opening his eyes to the rainbow's glow,
Mingo Mango's final wish
had come true!
And, it was so!

When Mingo Mango's
wishes were complete,
he looked toward the sky.

But the magic rainbow had
disappeared,
and never said goodbye.

Vele Keyta Y. Redding is a gifted storyteller, who melds the magic of imagination and wonder of words together to bring joy, laughter, awe and discovery to the hearts and minds of young readers. A professional journalist, author, content creator and media dynamo, Vele Keyta brings to life and her work messages of momentum, catapulting those around her to cast their nets wider and fly their kites higher. Her work on a plethora of subjects is published domestically and internationally. This is the first of several children's books she plans to publish. She lives in Atlanta with her husband and son.

Made in the USA
Middletown, DE
11 July 2017